NAVIGATING THROUGH

THE EXPERIENCES OF THE BARBER JOURNEY

Marquel Powell

ISBN 979-8-218-58933-2 Paperback

Navigating through the Experiences of the Barber Journey

This guide explores the art of barbering, offering diverse insights and viewpoints in the barber profession. It emphasizes the importance of a positive mindset, encouraging barbers to expect success and embrace all outcomes as opportunities for growth.

DEDICATION

I want to dedicate this book to my ambitious, energetic, adventurist, full of jokes and laughter kids: Dontavious, Caila, Journei, Jaycee.

I also want to dedicate this book to my sister, Marquita, and my brother, Elliott, who have always been important and valuable pieces of my life from behind the scenes, sharing positivity and honesty with me, propelling my journey in life forward.

To my beautiful, amazing, and beloved mother

Brenda E. Powell

ACKNOWLEDGEMENTS

I want to express my deepest gratitude to the barbershops that welcomed me into their space, giving me the opportunity to grow within this craft. Being part of your family, learning from your wisdom, and sharpening my skills under your guidance has been invaluable. Your mentorship not only shaped me as a barber but also inspired me to pass that knowledge on to the next generation. Now, as I step into the role of a mentor myself, I carry forward the lessons, discipline, and passion instilled in me. Thank you for being an essential part of my journey.

EDITOR'S NOTES

With two decades of experience in the barbering industry, I have navigated the highs, the challenges, and the ever-evolving craft that defines this journey. This book reflects of that path a truthful and concise collection of experiences designed to offer fresh perspectives on both technique and mindset. My goal is to equip barbers with the insight needed to approach their careers with confidence, adaptability, and a vision for success. Whether you are just starting out or sharpening your expertise, this book serves as a guide to achieving positive outcomes while embracing the full spectrum of the barbering experience.

Contents

The Path in Hindsight

Growing up, unaware of our limited means at the time, I now see how those early experiences built my resilience and shaped my work ethic. Looking back, I remember hearing "no" or "maybe later" whenever I asked for something. If I couldn't have it right away, I simply went back to playing, we didn't ask "why" by the next day, I'd usually forgotten about it anyway.

But I was wealthy in other ways. I was wealthy when it came to company. I was wealthy in terms of family, friends, and community, a place where everyone knew each other.

I also spent a lot of time with extended family and friends. I learned a lot from my uncles, older cousins, peers, and older gentlemen in the neighborhood especially on the front porch. I'd sit on a kitchen chair get my haircut with a towel draped around my shoulders, a window fan propped on a bucket blowing the hair clippings away. One set of clippers tweaked with a screwdriver and oiled with a few drops of 3-in-1 from red-and-white can handled the fade and line-up.

My mom and family members often said, "You know your grandmother gave you your first haircut., right?" I was too young to recall but I have two haircut stories I remember like yesterday. The first was when my mom gave me a haircut for my elementary school May Field Day event.

She cut my initials, *M* and *P,* in the back of my head. The kids at school thought it was so cool. But the kids on the bus from my neighborhood thought differently. One of the kids said the *M* on the back of my head like it didn't know if it wanted to be upper case or lower case. Don't feel bad for me, I was firing out jokes too. It was just my turn to get hit with a couple of shots, man! That was one long bus ride home.

Let me pause for a moment and give you some advice: beware joking around shots can backfire fast, and you might end up as the punchline.

The second time came when my stepdad cut my hair. I should've known better. He'd only ever shaved his own head and buzzed my little brother's hair down to, almost nothing.

But I needed an emergency cut and I paid the price. My Gumby high on the left, low on the right ended up as a tiny patch on one side of my head. I grabbed the scissors, snipped it off, and put on a do-rag to start forming waves.

That was the first and last time he'd butcher my hair. But my little brother was still getting butchered. One day, I saw that it was time for my brother to get a haircut. So, I decided to sneak into my parents' room, grab my stepdad's supermarket clippers the ones with the thin braided cord and black carrying case and oiled their still-noisy blades. That was all I had to work with I sat my brother down and gave him my first cut: a high bald fade with a part straight-line down the center, since the slanted part was already on its way out. That, haircut took forever because I had no trimmers to remove the bulk of the hair. I just had a clipper with no adjustment level only a screwdriver for the two screws to adjust the blades.

Still, I was proud of my first haircut. It was in no world the best, but it was definitely better than haircuts my brother had before. I remember my uncles and cousins asked who cut my brother's hair. I proudly told them I did. And that right there is where my barber journey begins. I started cutting hair on the front porch using a dining chair with a big towel and eventually made my way to Bishop State Community College's Barbering Program. I then went on to do an internship and to get my Master Barbering license while barbering at Pop's Barbershop.

Chapter Reflection Guide

1. Think of a childhood moment when you felt surrounded with love by family & friends. What made it meaningful, and how can you bring that feeling into other spaces today?

2. Describe a skill or passion you stumbled into by "just giving it a try," like I did when I picked up clippers. How has that first attempt shaped your path?

3. Looking back, how did limited resources push you to be creative? Where could that same mindset serve you today?

Decisions, Decisions, Decisions

When I first took up barbering, I kept my warehouse job for stability. I cut hair at the shop during the day focusing on walk-ins then worked a full evening shift at the warehouse.

Once my Tuesdays were full at the barbershop, I focused on filling the other days of the week one day at a time. Friday and Saturday were always the busiest, especially being the first barber in the shop and the last to leave. Over time, that helped me grow my clientele. Day by day, I took walk-ins while the other barbers stayed busy with their regulars. Between cuts, I sat in my chair, reading magazines and books there was no social media yet, and phones could barely take a decent photo; unlimited talk and text was the big selling point. Discipline, focus, and consistency made the transition smooth. Within a few months, I'd cut my warehouse job to part-time and was already earning more in the barbershop.

Eventually, I was able to quit that job and be a full-time master barber being my own CEO, manager, marketer, consultant, and assistant, getting my worth and value from the work I put in.

Looking back,

I can now say that set up was perfect for me. I had to make the decision that was best for me and the responsibilities I carried because no one else fully understood my situation like I did. I appreciated external options, but I had to trust myself to do what felt right from within.

Chapter Reflection Guide

1. What's one way you can attract more clients this week?

2. How much would you need to make each week to focus fully on barbering, and what is one step you will take to get there?

3. Think back to when you trusted your own voice over someone else's advice? How did it turn out and how can you use that moving forward?

No Easy Decisions

Moving from Alabama to Georgia was a big and painful decision because it meant I wasn't able to see my son and daughter throughout the week. I wasn't able to take them to school and spend quality time with them whenever I wanted.

Alabama was only four hours away practically next door, but I hadn't come to Georgia to mess around. With a few referrals, I visited several shops and met their owners. I didn't just look for the closest spot; I spent days driving by each shop in the morning, afternoon, and evening, watching the traffic and trying to figure out the vibe.

Eventually I chose Natural Blend/Tru Skills Barbershop and introduced to *Barbers Only Magazine the original source that put real barber culture on the map before social media, it was the platform that told our stories, showed our skills, and gave barbers real recognition. It wasn't just a magazine; it was a movement.* Ten years, I drove an hour each way, passing dozens of other shops, and never once regretted it. A decade later, I'm still on my barber journey now at Dre & Craig's VIP Cuts Barbershop.

Chapter Reflection Guide

1. What are you prepared to sacrifice whether it's your time or, your comfort, to pursue your barbering journey and the opportunities that align with your goals?

2. List four signs a barbershop is the perfect match for you (vibe, traffic, owners, growth potential).

3. What daily or weekly routine will help you stay dedicated to your craft?

Foundation

Establishing a solid foundation is essential for success and a sense of security, especially in barbering. If you know you overspend on fast food, impulse buys, and entertainment and struggle to save, it's time to change those habits and start putting money aside. I know from experience that saving a certain percentage of your earnings might not seem like much, but saving every day can accumulate into a powerful investment in your future, creating mountains of opportunities in other lanes for passive income.

As a new barber earning *cash every day, it's easy to fall into the trap of thinking, I will just make it back tomorrow, I will come in early or stay late.* But if you don't pause to assess your responsibilities, that cycle never ends. You are not getting any younger; every day you skip investing in yourself; you steal from your future. So, commit to investing in yourself every single day.

Chapter Reflection Guide

1. What's one spending habit you'll cut back on this week, and how much could you save?

2. Starting tomorrow, what exact percent or dollar amount from each cut will you commit to saving? What's the bigger goal behind it?

3.

4. That saved money is more than just cash its fuel. Will you invest it in tools, training, or something that earns while you cut building long term income?

Valuing Time

If you want clients who respect your schedule, start by respecting theirs. Show up on time and never take someone else's time for granted. When walk-ins and regulars notice this habit of yours, they will value it too. Many people have tight schedules and need to be in and out exactly within the slot shown on your booking app. So, honor it and don't budge.

If you're serious about long-term financial independence, use the downtime between cuts to invest in yourself. Read books, listen to audiobooks, study investing short bursts of learning each day add up quickly. Sit outside the shop or in your car and train your mind with material on discipline, focus, and consistency. The more knowledge you take in, the better you will recognize useful ideas in everyday conversations and the better questions you will ask the experts around you.

Chapter Reflection Guide

1. What habit can you build to make sure every cut starts right on time?

2. How will you use 15 minutes tomorrow into something that builds your future?

3. Name one solid rule you will put in place to make sure your schedule is valued just as much as your client's time.

Keep Your Schedule Tight

Barbering with a booking system is like operating and managing a company. Every minute counts and every decision sets the tone for the day. I learned early on that if you let anyone and everyone walk in without an appointment or call you up last minute, you end up drowning in chaos. It's like trying to run a race while carrying a backpack full of bricks. When you insist on online bookings, you're taking back control. Think of it like a credit score that reflects your responsibility: clients who schedule ahead show they respect your time, and in return, they pay your standard price no extra fees, no hidden surprises. They understand that their spot is earned, not given away like spare change on the street. It might feel like you're being rigid at first, but setting those boundaries is what keeps your business sustainable. Once you allow walk-ins or last-minute calls, the system starts to crumble. You begin working overtime just to keep up with the unexpected rush. And before you know it, you are constantly running late, struggling to honor appointments you had set in stone.

Meanwhile, the clients who booked online the ones who play by the rules get sidelined by the scramble. It's a lose-lose situation that chips away at your credibility and energy. Online bookings aren't just a scheduling tool; they're a signal to your customers about how you run your business. They show that you value efficiency, planning, and mutual respect. Clients who book online are like prime credit rating: they get the best rates and the smoothest experience. On the flip side, those who drop by unannounced or call at the last minute expecting the same VIP treatment must pay extra. It's not all about charging more; it's about reminding them that your time is valuable. It's the same principle you would see at a bank or credit bureau: responsible behavior has its rewards.

Of course, life isn't black and white. You will come across situations where a client might genuinely struggle with the booking app or a senior citizen who doesn't have access to schedule online. In these moments, a little flexibility goes a long way. But over time, you will learn to sift through the noise. Your experiences will sharpen your judgment, helping you recognize who respects your system and who's trying to game it. By sticking to a clear, online-first policy, you protect not only your schedule but also the quality of service you deliver. This isn't just about managing appointments; it's about preserving your passion for the craft and ensuring that every customer who steps into the shop knows they're getting the best you have to offer.

Chapter Reflection Guide

1. Where does your day tend to slip off track, and what simple fix could bring it back in line?

2. What clear expectation can I set around booking, timing, or late arrivals so clients understand that? And how can I show them I value their time just as much as mine?

3. Name one situation where you might make an exception to your rules, like helping a client who struggles with technology or dealing with a true emergency. How will you make sure that flexibility stays rare and doesn't become your new normal?

The Power of "NO" and Mastering Last Minute Chaos

In the fast- paced world, it's easy to get caught up in the expectation of always being available. Friends, regulars, and even a few new faces sometimes feel like they deserve an instant hook up, a quick cut without waiting. But here's the truth: being at everyone's disposal is not a badge of honor; it's a fast track to burnout. Over time, you will come to see that saying no is not just necessary; it's a form of respect for yourself and for the clients who plan. There's a rhythm that you must learn to navigate, and part of that rhythm is knowing when to shut the door.

When those last-minute calls come in, expect a mix of urgency and entitlement. Some will be real emergencies, and others are simply hoping to score a spot like they're your personal homeboy or homegirl. It's important to draw the line. Not every cry for help calls for immediate action. You might have to tell a client, "I'm booked up for today, let's schedule you for tomorrow." That simple act of setting a boundary can eventually steer them toward booking online. Over time, as you consistently enforce your rules, the people who truly need you will learn that your schedule is not up for grabs on a whim.

There's a certain freedom in owning your schedule. It means you're not letting the unexpected throw your day into chaos. When you decide in advance that online bookings get priority, you're not just protecting your time; you're also ensuring that the quality of service doesn't drop because you're stretched too thin. Clients who insist on calling at the last minute might get an occasional exception, but if you let it become the norm, you risk blurring the lines between true emergencies and casual conveniences. It's a slippery slope that leads to overwork and under-delivery.

Learning to say no might feel like you're turning away people, but it's about making sure that the ones who count get what they deserve. It's about maintaining a balance where you're not only meeting expectations but exceeding them for those who invest in the process. It's a mindset that respects both the craft and your personal well-being. When you're not constantly scrambling to fill unexpected gaps, you can focus on what matters most: delivering top-notch service to those who understand the value of planning ahead.

Ultimately, the goal is to create a system where the right clients gravitate toward the right process. It's about building a reputation where your time is seen as precious and your schedule, a well-oiled machine. With each call you decline and each appointment you schedule in advance, you're carving out more space to do what you love without compromise. And as you navigate through the noise of last-minute demands, you'll find that maintaining those boundaries not only keeps you on time but also elevates the overall experience for everyone involved.

Chapter Reflection Guide

1. When have you felt pressure to take a client you didn't plan for? How might a clear "no" have helped you protect your time and quality?

2. Recall a situation when you *did* accept a last-minute request. How did it affect your schedule, stress level, and the client's appreciation? What insight does that give you about when to say "no"?

3. Imagine your ideal workday one year from now. How would having boundaries shape who you are professionally and the kind of clients you attract?

Morning Habits

I have a morning ritual that I don't stray from. When the sun rises, I turn off my cell phone ringer because I know everybody is safe and doing well my kids, family, and friends. Then, I sit on the edge of the bed for a few minutes counting my blessings, thankful to be here to effectively support my health, family, and friends.

After finishing my hygiene routine, I do some stretching exercises and meditate by an open window, letting the sunlight stimulate alpha-wave activity. Because I lay out my clothes the night before a habit, I picked up from books on building positive routines and reducing decision fatigue I can get dressed quickly. I always keep a book on the sofa and challenge myself each morning to recall what I read the night before and apply at least one of its principles during the day. On the drive to the barbershop, I listen to audiobooks. These morning habits sharpen my mindset, helping me make better decisions throughout the day and delivering cumulative benefits over time.

Chapter Reflection Guide

1. If you could choose just one way to ground your mourning, would it be gratitude, a good stretch, or quiet reading, and why does that speak to you?

____
____
____
____
____
____
____

2. Think of one thing you can prepare the evening before, whether it is your outfit, tools, or your first meal. How might that help you start the day with more focus and clarity?

____
____
____
____
____
____
____

3. After a week of your new morning routine, what changes big or small do you notice in your mood, energy, or client interactions?

____
____
____
____
____
____
____

Embracing the Process

Barbering is all about consistency and discipline the process is a marathon, not a quick sprint. Don't get discouraged or impatient on your barbering journey. We all started from a place of not knowing and had to grind to figure things out, mastering the skills while collecting bumps and bruises and earning our stripes along the way. Only in hindsight do you see how the dots connect.

Trust and believe, I wrecked plenty of haircuts in the beginning. I would hand people the mirror and think to myself, *I know I'm not getting paid for this,* a.k.a. the butcher cut. The worst were the barbershop regular walk in's who didn't care which barber gave them a haircut. After the cut, they would hang around for hours, and I knew the other barbers could see every mistake, giving me that respectful smirk that said, "I remember those days."

I once worked in a shop where we would make bird calls whenever a cut was off point. It was all in genuine fun only the barbers knew. Looking back, I figured some clients had to been insane or blind, because they kept coming back week after week and waiting to sit in my chair, even when the veteran barbers were sometimes available.

But every time I cut their hair, I got a little better, learning from the mistakes I made from my client's previous visit. They were trusting me with their image, and I was determined to give them the best one possible. Ask any barber about their beginnings one hundred percent of us have horror stories.

When you're in the shop with veteran barbers, remember, we were once in your shoes. Don't pick up bad habits getting impatient, rushing through cuts, or trying to scoop up every walk-in. Don't be that barber who just draped a client while telling a new arrival, "You're next; it'll only take me fifteen minutes," when you haven't even started the head in your chair. Clients and walk-ins notice your service. They might not say a word, but if you walk into the shop one day and see two or three of your regulars in other barber chairs, it stings and afterward, they'll ask for the other barber's booking info.

Don't rush the process. You can't get there in a single day. It takes time to build relationships with existing clients and walk-ins.

When I started, there were no social media tutorials nor any insight about the barber industry just observing other barbers, hair shows, barbering textbook, *Barbers Only Magazine*, and *W.Y.B. Magazine.* I learned to minimize errors as time went on, and I never turn down any hair texture I was just determined to get better. In my downtime, I'd watch the veteran barbers, mesmerized by the magic they worked with a pair of clippers, studying every move until I could memorize their skills. I can still picture myself flicking on my own clippers, holding them in my hand, staring into the mirror over my station, and saying, "That's going to be me one day." What I always saw in those vets was discipline, consistency, reliability men who kept their word.

You must build the right mindset over time. The barbershop will throw all kinds of challenges at you, but they don't arrive all at once some lessons reveal themselves only after years behind the chair. That's why a positive outlook is crucial. Not every day will be good, and some mornings, you will not want to open the shop and some evening you will not want to close the shop. When that happens, remember how far you have come whether you started in a garage, on a front porch, or in a spare bedroom. Take it one haircut at a time, one day at a time. Mastering this industry is a lifelong journey, and it's always evolving with new trends.

Chapter Reflection Guide

1. What did your most challenging cut teach you about your craft or your growth?

2. What is one thing a skilled barber does that stands out to you, and how can you bring that into your own routine this week?

3. When you feel the urge to rush what small action can help you slow down and focus on one haircut at a time?

Despite it All

Despite my ups and downs, I'm grateful and blessed to wake up every morning with good health and strength. I never want to feel ungrateful sometimes disappointments, setbacks, and challenges in life take a toll on us in unique ways. Watching and listening to the local news or worldwide media in the barbershop can have you feeling like the world is on the brink of chaos, with nothing but negativity surrounding us. However, I choose to see life through a different lens one of gratitude. I'm thankful for the opportunities I've been given and strive, to maximize my gifts and talents every day.

My goals are to be of service to others, both inside and outside the barbershop, and to contribute to the solution rather than the problem. I'm so appreciative of my grandmother, my mom, uncles, aunts, cousins, and the community around me that I grew up in, because I got a chance to see the people in my environment maximize what they had with less resources and less opportunities. I take no day for granted. Every day, I make a conscious decision to work on myself to be better than who I was yesterday, constantly striving to improve with decisions and choices in life.

I don't like asking myself if I could have done more to maximize my time. I'm so grateful and blessed to be a master barber. I don't take my talents, skills, and abilities for granted. I don't treat barbering like a side hustle to make a few dollars to get through the day. I treat it as a profession; with the respect and dedication it deserves.

Chapter Reflection Guide

1. List three good things in your life right now, even the small ones.

2. What is one simple way you can help someone today, inside or outside the shop?

3. Name one habit or choice you will improve tomorrow so you keep growing.

Continuous Learning

The first step is always sanitation. After that, get familiar with your clippers learn the lever positions, memorize the guard system, and know exactly which guard and lever setting create each blend from one guideline to the next. Master one clipper inside and out before you start mixing brands. If you can't tell a regular blade from a fade blade, or steel from ceramic, or understand how different motors cut, you are building on shaky ground. The fundamentals are everything. Stay consistent, study every step of every haircut on every texture, and stack that knowledge one cut at a time. Enjoy the journey; later you will see every struggle was part of the process. There are no shortcuts in this game.

Once your basics are tight, invest in some basic content creation equipment. The right camera, clean lighting, and a solid background, and your photos and reels will take your social-media marketing to the next level, showing the world the quality of your work.

Chapter Reflection Guide

1. How will you fit 10 minutes of study or practice into every workday, so your skills never stop growing?

____
____
____
____
____
____
____

2. What skill or tool are you still working to master and how will you commit to improving it?

____
____
____
____
____
____
____

3. What is one new technique or detail you want to learn next to help your work stand out?

____
____
____
____
____
____
____

Encountering Challenges

Barbers, if you're struggling to pass the licensing exam and the shop owner or other barbers are going the extra mile offering study material, advice, or hands-on coaching take it. They have the experience and know what the test demands; listening could help you on something you missed. Remember, the owner is taking a risk by letting an unlicensed barber work. In many states, the first penalty is about $500, and the second can reach $1,000. Don't put the shop in jeopardy by cutting corners. You don't want to be that barber who spots a white car with a state seal, and take off running for the break room, leaving a half-finished client in the chair while another barber scrambles to complete the cut. It's a bad look for everyone. Respect the opportunity, study hard, and get that Master Barber license.

Chapter Reflection Guide

1. Who around you shop owner, coworkers, friends can give you study tips or practice time, and how will you ask for it?

____
____
____
____
____
____
____

2. What is one clear step you will add to your routine this week (flash cards, mock test, hands-on drills) to get closer to passing the exam?

____
____
____
____
____
____
____

3. How will earning your license on time show respect for the shop, your teammates, and the clients who trust you?

____
____
____
____
____
____
____

Barbering On Off Days

Off-days can get tricky in this trade. Most barbers keep a regular schedule, but every now and then, we must pop in on what's usually a day off sometimes for an emergency cut or prioritize clients in before a trip. When that happens, some of us send a mass text weeks or days in advance: "I'll be in the shop next Monday from 10 a.m. to 2 p.m. only." Spell it out, because clients may assume those new hours are permanent and just show up unannounced no text, no call hoping you're there.

If a client needs a cut for something important and you're off and every other barber is booked they might head back to their old shop or find a new one that fits their schedule better. Clear, consistent communication about workdays, off days, and one-off "special opening" days keeps expectations straight and loyalty intact. I remind myself never to take a single client for granted; they pass multiple barbershops to sit in my chair.

Chapter Reflection Guide

1. How will you tell clients clearly and early when you'll be in the shop on a normal day off?

2. How will you make sure extra appointments don't crowd out the personal time you need to recharge?

3. How does taking time off recharge both your body and mind?

Being Mindful

A barbershop should feel like a second home, a community, and a space where respect should be the foundation of everything we do. When working with female barbers, it's not about making exceptions or treating them differently; it's about recognizing their talent, dedication, and role as equals in the craft. Everyone in the shop is there for the same purpose: to sharpen skills, build a clientele, and create an environment where both barbers and clients feel comfortable. The energy we bring to work affects everyone, and when there's unity and professionalism, the shop thrives. No one should feel overlooked, disrespected, or out of place in a profession built on personal connections. If we wouldn't want our grandmothers, mothers, sisters, or daughters to experience disrespect in their workplaces, then why allow it in our own? Being mindful of how we treat each other is about setting a standard that strengthens the industry.

When barbers, regardless of gender, feel valued and respected, the entire shop operates at a higher level, creating a space where everyone can succeed and grow together.

When women and kids are in the barbershop, be mindful of conversations, music, and tv shows, all of which should be free of inappropriate language and content even though some clients probably hear and see it with their kids. I would rather be the change creating a positive environment versus talking about who is going to start the change we want to see.

Chapter Reflection Guide

1. What simple action can you take today to show every coworker that you value them?

2. How will you manage things like music, conversation, and TV to help keep the space family friendly?

3. Imagine a loved one stepping into your shop. How can you create an environment that would make them feel respected and comfortable?

Different skills, one strong shop

Adding a hairstylist & loctician to the team turns the shop into a genuine one-stop grooming studio. Her clients can slide over for a fresh fade; your regulars can book a retwist without leaving the building. That steady back-and-forth keeps both schedules full and widens the shop's reach with almost no extra effort.

The payoff extends beyond extra appointments. Families appreciate handling every hair need in one visit, and the shop's reputation grows as the place that can do it all cuts, and retwists, under a single roof. Convenience deepens loyalty, and everyone behind the chair's benefits.

Chapter Reflection Guide

1. What extra skill or partner could you add to create a true one-stop shop for your clients?

____
____
____
____
____
____
____
____

2. How would this new service save clients time and keep them loyal to your shop?

____
____
____
____
____
____
____
____

3. What simple step will you take this week sign, post, text to tell people about the added service?

____
____
____
____
____
____
____

Daily Self Investing

Some game-changing reads belong on every barber's shelf or in your earbuds: self-improvement, spiritual growth, and mindset books. I soak them up in every format paperback, e-book, audiobook because the people who wrote them already paid the price in sweat and study. Their sacrifice becomes my shortcut.

The best money lesson I ever pulled from that stack is "pay yourself first." I peel off a set percentage of every dollar, every single day, not just when I have extra to spare and channel it into investments. If the right mentors aren't in your neighborhood, create the environment: YouTube University and Patreon groups sit in the palm of your hand. Thanks to solid educators online, I've learned to make calm, patient moves in the stock market with that "pay-yourself-first" cash.

When a client dozes off in my chair, I'm in class headphones on, soaking up podcasts on self-development, credit strategy, and financial literacy. That's how I nailed the finer points of due dates, reporting dates, reward points, and even the smaller credit bureaus most people ignore (shout-out to ATL Chill for the gem on freezing those). Monday and Tuesday nights I'm on live YouTube shows breaking down balance sheets; Sundays I'm studying technical analysis; and a mentor-turned-client is walking me through the futures market. The books lit the spark, but the daily discipline keeps the fire burning.

When I'm cutting one of my mentors, the talk starts with a quick check-in family good, life good then shifts straight to the markets: current moves, long-term plays, and the goals. Once a week we fire up Zoom so he can walk me through the futures market, chart by chart. Another regular client who works for an Atlanta airline brings the same energy; every session, we trade notes on our portfolios, break down strategies, and look ahead to where the next wave of opportunity might land.

When my client the real-estate investor from Arizona or my client the real-estate agent out of New York slides into my chair, the talk swaps from stocks to property plays what they've just closed on, why the numbers make sense, and which markets I should scout next. The puzzle pieces are everywhere; cut the background noise so you can tune in. Create a space that feeds your mindset read, listen, and learn every day. Lay one brick at a time, track every layer, and you will build a foundation solid enough to share and lead by example.

Back when I dug into credit, I discovered the game doesn't stop at the big three bureaus. Those secondary bureaus also feed data upstream, so I called each one, froze my files, or shut them off from reporting. After that, I fired off dispute letters and settled the newer collections instead of waiting out the clock. Once a dispute sticks, always cross-check all three major bureaus to confirm the item vanished everywhere. Whenever I paid a collection, I got it in writing that the account would be removed, not just marked "paid." That move alone started my climb to a higher score and a bigger credit line in under 36 months.

Now I work my cards instead of dodging them. I know every opening date, due date, and closing date; keep utilization low and pay the balance in full before the statement cuts. Offers pour in through apps, email, and snail mail. Cash from haircuts hits the bank, a set percentage slides straight into my Roth IRA, and the rest might land in a high-yield CD. Even the teller notices suddenly I'm getting low-rate loan and business-card offers because I'm simply doing the grown-up routine, I've always done paying the water, lights, internet, and phone bills only now they run through one credit card that's paid off monthly. Just that tweak sent my score soaring.

Most days I'm locked into INTJ mode head down between cuts, researching, testing innovative ideas, and sharing the results with anyone who wants the game. When the convo starts firing on all cylinders, I flip to ENTJ I pull the gems from every discussion, plug them into my system, and keep tweaking the formula. Whatever I didn't know yesterday becomes today's upgrade steady compound growth for both my craft and my mindset.

And how does it relate to the art of being a barber? Barbering is more than just cutting hair it's also running a small business. Because you only earn what you cut, money skills set right beside your clippers. Good credit lets you grab new tools, upgrade your station, or even sign a lease on your own shop when you're ready. A habit of paying yourself first builds a cushion, so slow weeks don't knock you off balance and you're not sweating rent when walk-in traffic is not constant. Investing that cushion whether in stocks, real estate, or a Roth IRA sets you up for life after the chair, so you're not still grinding out thirty heads a day at seventy. And when you can drop a quick tip on fixing credit or saving cash. Paying yourself first becomes another mindset tool in your kit, keeping the business strong today and securing your future tomorrow.

Chapter Reflection Guide

1. Choose one book, podcast, or video series you'll finish this month. What do you hope it teaches you?

2. Choose one financial move that makes sense for you whether it is starting a Roth IRA, freezing credit, or automating a bill. Write down the exact date you will do it and your first step.

3. How will you measure your personal growth with something like a journal, spreadsheet, or app? Start by drafting your first note today.

Collaboration Over Competition

In the barber industry, it's easy to fall into the trap of competition seeing every barbershop or barber around you as a rival. But let's take a step back and look at the bigger picture. The reality is this: there are far more people in your community than there are barbers to serve them.

Think about the population of your city or town. Now, compare that number to the number of barbershops and barbers in the area. Could you or even every barber in your city combined serve every single person in your community on a daily, weekly, or even monthly basis? The load would be impossible for one barber, one shop, or even a handful of shops to handle.

This realization is freeing because it highlights a simple truth: there's no need to compete. The demand for quality barbers far outweighs the supply. Instead of focusing on what others are doing, focus on serving your clients to the best of your ability.

Let's crunch the numbers. Say your city has a population of one hundred thousand people. If fifty percent of them gets haircuts regularly, that's fifty thousand potential clients. Now, let's assume there are fifty barbers in your city. That's one thousand potential clients per barber. Could you realistically cut one thousand heads in a week? Even if every barber worked nonstop, it would be impossible to meet that demand.

So, instead of competing for clients, we can focus on building strong relationships with the clients we have? Provide excellent service, stay consistent, and let your work speak for itself.

At the same time, encourage others in the industry to do the same. The more skilled and respected barbers there are in a community benefits and the more value the profession gains.

Focus on providing an experience so exceptional that your clients choose you not because there's no other option, but because they value the care, precision, and atmosphere you provide.

Chapter Reflection Guide

1. How does knowing there are more potential clients than any one barber can serve shift your attitude toward other barbers?

2. Name one barber or shop you respect. How could you team up (share tips, refer overflow clients, run a joint promo) so you both win?

3. What extra effort or small gesture will you use to make sure clients return because they appreciate how you treat them?

Ego

Ego will have you out here thinking you have to outshine everybody, that you have to move like there's not enough to go around because there is. Too many barbers move with a scarcity mindset, thinking every client, ever dollar, every opportunity is slipping through their fingers. That kind of thinking leads to stress, burnout, and unnecessary drama. But when you switch to an abundance mindset, you start to realize the right people will find you. Your style, your vibe, your skills those are what attract clients who connect with you. Instead of worrying about what the next barber is doing, put that energy into sharpening your craft and giving your clients an experience they can't get anywhere else.

Barbers who move with abundance don't see other barbers as threats; they see them as part of the culture. When one of us wins, the whole industry levels up. Instead of beefing over clients, build connections, share game, and push each other to be better. That energy? It comes back full circle. You show love, you get love. Clients respect barbers that move with confidence, not desperation if you stay focused, put in work, and trust that there's always more coming, you will never have to chase because opportunities will come knocking.

Chapter Reflection Guide

1. In what area do you feel a lack whether it is clients, income, or recognition? Write one mindset shift you can make to see opportunity instead.

____

____

____

____

____

____

____

2. Who is one barber you'll lift up or learn from this week, and how will you take that step?

____

____

____

____

____

____

____

3. How does the experience in your chair differ from the rest, and what will you do to highlight that strength?

____

____

____

____

____

____

____

Barbering is About Community

Barbering has always been about community. Historically, barbershops have been a gathering place, and safe space where people come not just for haircuts but for connection, conversation, and camaraderie. When we collaborate rather than compete, we strengthen those roots.

Sharing tips with other barbers, refer clients to colleagues if your schedule is full. Small acts like these not only build trust but also create a ripple effect of positivity in the industry. Together, we can ensure that every client in the community is served, and that barbering continues to thrive as both a craft and a culture.

Chapter Reflection Guide

1. What is one small thing you can do so people feel welcome to hang out and talk, not just get a haircut?

____
____
____
____
____
____
____

2. When your schedule is full, how can you turn a missed opportunity into support for a teammate and still give the client a great experience?

____
____
____
____
____
____
____

3. What's one-way that sharing your skills or clients now could lead to stronger bonds and long-term success for everyone around you?

____
____
____
____
____
____
____

Supporting Barbers on Their Journey

As a barbershop owner, one of the most rewarding aspects of the business is watching barbers grow not just as professionals but as individuals with dreams and aspirations of their own. Every barber starts somewhere: behind a chair in someone else's shop, perfecting their craft, and learning the ins and outs of the industry. But for many barbers, there comes a time when they feel called to take a leap of faith, to spread their wings and venture out on their own.

When this moment comes, it's important for shop owners to embrace it as a natural and necessary part of the barber journey. Rather than seeing it as a loss, see it as a milestone in the relationship you have built with that barber. Congratulate them, celebrate their courage, and honor the role you have played in helping them get to this point.

Chapter Reflection Guide

1. When a teammate decides to move on, what thoughts come to mind, and how can you turn that moment into something supportive?

2. Think about the next generation coming up behind you. What could you share to make their next big move smoother?

3. What is one sign that your workplace truly supports personal growth, and how will you make that signal stronger?

From Mentorship to Legacy

Being a shop owner is more than just renting chairs and managing schedules; it's about fostering an environment where barbers can grow. Whether it's helping them get licensed, giving them a space to learn the ropes, or sharing industry knowledge, your role as a mentor can leave a lasting impact.

But mentorship doesn't come with strings attached. The barbers who work in your shop aren't obligated to stay for their entire careers. Just as you once moved on from someone else's shop to create your own path, your barbers may eventually feel the pull to do the same. It's a cycle that keeps the barber culture alive and thriving.

Instead of holding them back, encourage them to follow their dreams. After-all, their success reflects the foundation you helped build. When a barber leaves your shop to open their own or take on new challenges, it's a testament to the environment you provided an environment where growth was not only possible but inevitable.

Because when you provide a space for barbers to grow, you're doing more than running a business; you're creating a legacy. Every barber who passes through your shop carries a piece of that legacy with them. The knowledge, skills, and confidence they gain under your roof will ripple outward as they mentor the next generation of barbers.

In this way, the work you do as a shop owner goes far beyond the day-to-day operations. You're contributing to the future of the industry one barber at a time. And when those barbers go on to open their own shops or find success in nontraditional setups, it's not a loss it's a win for the industry.

So, keep in mind that being a part of a barber's journey is a privilege. Not every shop owner takes the time to invest in their barbers, but those who do leave a lasting mark on the industry. When you see a barber, you mentored go on to achieve great things, it's a reminder of the ripple effect of your work.

The barbering journey is not a solo endeavor; it's a shared experience, built on the support, knowledge, and encouragement of those who came before. As a shop owner, you could have the opportunity to be part of that legacy. Celebrate it, honor it, and continue to pass it on.

Chapter Reflection Guide

1. What's the one thing you hope people you've trained will remember most about working with you?

____
____
____
____
____
____
____

2. Name one skill or tip you can share this week that could help someone long after they leave your shop.

____
____
____
____
____
____
____

3. Picture a barber you've mentored ten years from now. What would make you proud to hear them say about your influence?

____
____
____
____
____
____
____

A New Era in Barbering

The barbering industry is evolving. Traditionally, barbershops followed a specific model: fixed stations, set schedules, and a close-knit group of barbers under one roof. But, today, barbers are exploring new ways of working.

From renting private suites and office spaces to sharing units in flea markets, barbers are finding innovative ways to serve their clients. These setups often come with fewer overhead cost no water bills, no internet fees, no electric bills, and more flexibility. Some shops are even redefining traditional models, and schedules.

As a shop owner, it's important to recognize and adapt to these changes. The barbers' you mentor may decide to step outside the traditional barbershop model, and that's okay. The industry is big enough to accommodate all kinds of setups, and these shifts reflect the creativity and adaptability that make barbering such a dynamic profession.

Chapter Reflection Guide

1. Picture yourself in your ideal work environment. Is it a private suite, a shared space, or a traditional barbershop? Which setup fits your style best, and why?

2. What bills or rules would you gladly drop, and what trade-offs might come with that freedom?

3. What's one step you could take to adapt to the industry's new ways of working?

Bridging the Gap

Barbering is a universal craft, yet language, terminology, and expectations around haircuts that can really vary depending on where a client is from. A taper in one city might mean something entirely different in another city. A temp fade could have different interpretations based on the region, ethnicity, or even the shop culture a client is used to. These differences can sometime make things a little challenging.

This is where visual communication becomes a game changer. In an industry built on precision, relying only on verbal descriptions can sometimes lead to misunderstanding and that's the last thing you want as you build your clientele. A client may ask for a specific cut, but if their definition of that style differs from the barber's, it can result in frustration, disappointment, and ultimately, a negative experience.

Pictures and videos cut through the confusion. Instead of guessing what a client means by "just a little off the top," have them pull up a shot on Instagram, Pinterest, or TikTok. One glance at that reference photo and you're both locked on the same target no dissatisfied response when the barber spins the client toward the mirror to see the haircut.

These visual clips help us behind the chair, too. Scroll YouTube or Instagram and you'll see how different regions shape the same cut. The more visuals you stash in your head, the more confident you'll be when any style, and any hair type walks through the door.

And if at any point in your career, you see a fellow barber making a similar mistake, step in and clear up any confusion if you can. In these situations, you have two options:

1. **Step in and help**. Offer your knowledge, provide clarity, or suggest a visual reference to help guide the consultation.
2. **Stay silent and watch them fail**. Allow them to struggle through the misunderstanding, knowing that it could result in a dissatisfied client walking out the door.

If you choose the second option remaining silent and internally cheering for their failure, you're not just hurting that barber; you're hurting the entire shop. Every client who walks out unhappy doesn't just blame the barber who cut their hair. They may judge the entire shop and choose not to come back again.

At the end of the day, barbering is a craft that thrives on continuous learning and adaptation. The more barbers understand and respect regional and cultural differences in haircut terminology, the more they can serve a diverse clientele with confidence. Supporting fellow barbers, rather than silently watching them struggle, helps the entire barbershop.

Barbering is bigger than one person it's about the community, the craft, and the culture. And when one barber gets better, we all get better.

Chapter Reflection Guide

1. Recall a time you and a client used the same words for a cut but pictured something different. What will you do next time to be sure you're both seeing the same style?

____

____

____

____

____

____

2. Name one haircut term that's commonly used but can be interpreted in various ways depending on where you are. How would you confirm its meaning with the client before you start.

____

____

____

____

____

____

____

3. If you see another barber headed for a mix-up, how will you step in, so the client and the shop still leave happy?

____

____

____

____

____

____

____

The Ripple Effect of a Bad Haircut

That being said, let's look at what it means to have a bad haircut and the long-term effect this can have. Think about how often people travel and get haircuts in different cities. A bad experience with one barber can lead to broad, sweeping judgments:

"Man, I went to a city, and none of those barbers can cut!"

I'll never get a cut in this state again. They messed me up."

But they didn't get a bad cut from an entire city or state. They had one bad experience with one barber. Yet that single experience can shape their perception of barbering in that entire area.

This is why it's crucial for barbers within a shop to look out for each other. A dissatisfied client doesn't just hurt one barber; it can lead to negative word of mouth that impacts everyone.

Chapter Reflection Guide

1. When have you seen (or heard about) a single bad cut hurting a shop's reputation? What lesson does that story give you?

2. What quick step like a mirror check, second opinion, or photo can you add to catch any mistakes before the client leaves your chair?

3. If a coworker's cut goes wrong, how can you step in kindly, so the client leaves satisfied, and the shop's name stays strong?

Kids in the Barber Chair

Every kid reacts differently in the barber's chair especially first-timers or those getting a big chop. Some are just nervous; others have sensory sensitivities, ADHD, or autism. The game plan is simple: patience, flexibility, and a big dose of empathy.

Before the clippers even buzz, strike up a convo. Ask about their favorite cartoon, superhero, or snack. That quick back-and-forth shifts the chair from "scary" to "safe."

Once they're talking, keep the vibe light. Crack a joke, hand them a fidget toy, or fire up their show on a tablet. If they're laughing or locked in on a cartoon, the cut goes smoother and everybody leaves smiling.

Ask parents if their child has specific triggers or preferences. They may be more comfortable with a certain routine. If the shop is too busy or loud offer the parents a quieter time the next visit, such as early morning or late evening.

Before you start cutting the child's hair, let the child feel the vibration of the clipper (if they're willing) just letting them know the clippers don't hurt. Cordless clippers and quiet trimmers can be helpful. If the child is hesitant, start with scissors instead of clippers. Gradually introduce clippers once they feel more at ease.

Some kids don't like the feeling of the neck strip or cape. If you can only get the neck strip on for the first visit, that's a start. Keep moving forward.

Many kids dislike hair being cut around their ears, neck, or forehead. Start with easier areas and work up to the more challenging areas.

Be patient with sudden movements. If a child flinches or moves, stop and reassure them before continuing.

Some kids need to pause to reset. Giving them a minute before you start up again can prevent a full meltdown.

Even if it takes longer than usual, maintaining a calm and encouraging demeanor helps build trust.

Patience is key when working with small kids. The goal isn't just to complete a haircut; it's to create a positive experience. Every small success, from sitting in the chair to tolerating the cape, is progress. When parents see that you genuinely care about making the experience positive for their child, they'll trust you more and keep coming back.

Chapter Reflection Guide

1. What questions will you ask parents (or the child) before the cut, so you understand any fears or sensory issues?

2. List one tool and one tactic you'll keep ready like a fidget toy, quiet clippers, or an early morning slot to help anxious kids feel safe.

3. After the cut, note one tiny success (tolerated the cape, sat still for the clippers). How will you use that win to make the next visit even smoother?

Exceptional Service for the Elderly Clients

Older clients are considered shop VIP gold members. Give them the extra comfort they need a steady arm, softer touch, a little more time and they'll leave feeling cared for and keep coming back. You'll see their name popping up on your schedule routinely.

Some elderly clients have mobility challenges, and making small adjustments can make a significant difference. For example, you can adjust the barber chair as needed, offer extra time to get seated, and be extra patient throughout the process.

If a client experiences difficulty transferring from a wheelchair to your barber chair, offer to remove the barber chair to create more space and to make the process smoother.

Some elderly clients might have walkers and canes helping them safely store their mobility aids during the appointment. Offer a steady arm when transition from their walker or scooter to the barber chair.

Helping elderly clients to their vehicle even if they don't ask, offering a steady hand while they walk out, holding the door open, or carrying small personal items can be greatly appreciated and can really improve the overall experience.

Elderly clients may struggle with online booking systems and smartphones. Being flexible and understanding can make their experience smoother.

Ask which day and time suits them best and slot it in yourself. If they're creatures of habit, lock in a weekly or bi-weekly spot and follow up with a quick call or text reminder. And stay flexible some elders will just drop by or send a family member to see if you're available.

If they don't text, encourage them to call the shop directly or have a family member call for them.

Take your time with older clients some walk slower, hear softer, or circle back to the same stories. Listen up and show real interest; that respect builds trust. Notice every detail as you go: the way they like the neckline squared, the warm-towel finish. Remember it next visit and you'll turn a simple trim into a relationship that lasts.

Some elderly clients may not have frequent social interactions, and your kindness can brighten their day. Many elderly clients have been coming to the same barber for decades. Recognizing their loyalty with small gestures like a discount or prioritizing them in your schedule reinforces their value to your shop.

Know the cut before they tell you. Greet them with: "Same as last time little off the top, tighter on the sides, lineup light around the edges?" That quick recall makes them feel remembered.

Then warm up the chair with genuine chat: "How's the family? Haven't seen you in a minute you had me about to put out an APB!" If they circle back to the same stories, lean in and laugh along. A little enthusiasm goes a long way.

Building a strong relationship with elderly clients isn't just about business. it's about making them feel respected, valued, and at home in your shop. The extra effort you put into personalizing their experience will lead to lifelong customers and even referrals from their friends and family.

Chapter Reflection Guide

1. What small change (slower pace, steady arm, warm facial towel) will you add to make an older client feel at ease?

____

____

____

____

____

____

____

2. How can you simplify scheduling for clients who don't text or use apps?

____

____

____

____

____

____

____

3. What simple method (note in your phone, appointment card, mental cue) will you use to track any client's preferences so you can personalize their next visit?

____

____

____

____

____

____

____

Responding, Not Reacting in the Shop

The barbershop is more than just a workplace; it's a cultural hub filled with personalities, conversations, and unpredictable situations. Mastering yourself in this environment means learning how to stay composed, adapt to different people, and not take things personally.

Any shift can bring a mix of personalities. You'll have the regulars who treat the shop like home and speak their minds. New faces might sit cautious and skeptical. Then come the loud, opinion-makers ready to spark a debate. Add in folks from every background, each with their own social norms, and you've got the daily barbershop lineup. Instead of seeing the barbershop as a chaotic or stressful place, view it as dynamic learning environment where you can sharpen your people skills, patience, and emotional control.

Tensions can rise over conversations, long wait times, or even small misunderstandings. Your ability to respond instead of reacting will define your professionalism.

Reacting is impulsive letting emotions take control without thinking.

Responding is intentional, where you process the situation, stay calm, and choose your words wisely.

Let's say a client complains about the price.

Wrong reaction: "That's the price, take it or leave it." (Sounds defensive and dismissive.)

Professional response: "I understand, and I appreciate your business. Our prices reflect the quality and time we put into each cut." (This keeps the conversation respectful and leaves no room for argument.)

A fellow barber challenges you in front of clients.
Wrong reaction: "Man, why you always got something to say?" (Escalates tension.)

Professional response: "I hear you. Let's talk about that later." (Shows maturity and keeps things from getting messy in front of clients.)

A client criticizes the haircut midway through.
Wrong reaction: Snapping back with frustration.
Professional response: "I appreciate the feedback. Let me know exactly what you're thinking so we can get it right." (Keeps the client involved and turns a negative experience into a positive one.)

Pause before you speak; it keeps you cool and steers you clear of pointless drama.

Chapter Reflection Guide

1. What quick habit (deep breath, silent count, smile) will help you stay calm when a client or coworker pushes your buttons?

2. Write in some respectful lines you can use the next time someone questions your price, skills, or opinion.

3. Think of a recent tense situation at work. How could a calm response rather than a snap reaction have changed the outcome?

Common Challenges & How to Handle Them

As a barber, you will inevitably face challenges and obstacles along the way. Since this isn't something, you can avoid within this profession or any profession, it's important to know how to deal with these situations when they arise.

Let's say a client request another barber. Instead of feeling disrespected, see it as a personal preference, not a reflection of your skills.

Some clients might be talkative. Some clients just want a quiet cut.

Shop debates might get heated. Barbershops are known for passionate discussions. Stay neutral if needed, and don't engage in unnecessary arguments.

Client's cancel last minute. If it happens, focus on the next client instead of dwelling on lost time.

If someone's energy is negative, its more about them than it is about you. Your job is to remain professional, not absorb their frustration.

Detach emotionally from situations. If something annoys you, ask yourself: *Will this matter tomorrow?*

Breathe before you speak. A deep breath can prevent a bad reaction.

Take breaks when needed. Step outside for a minute if you feel overwhelmed.

Keep your focus on growth. The calmer and more professional you are, the more respected and successful you'll become.

Chapter Reflection Guide

1. When a client cancels, asks for someone else, or brings bad energy, what simple rule will you follow to stay calm and move on?

____
____
____
____
____
____
____

2. Think of one small frustration from this week. Will it matter tomorrow? If not, how will you drop it?

____
____
____
____
____
____
____

3. How can keeping your cool during shop debates or tense moments help you earn more trust and success over time?

____
____
____
____
____
____
____

Ways to Adapt & Build Connections

Whoever lands in your chair faithful regulars or cautious first times should feel like they belong. That starts with cultural awareness: pick up the slang, customs, and social cues of the neighborhoods you serve so your conversation hits the right note.

While the clippers buzz, give clients more airtime than you take; a few minutes spent listening to their work stories or weekend plans does more for loyalty than any promotion.

As you talk, look for common ground sports scores, favorite artists, family milestones because a shared interest turns a routine trim into a friendly check-in. And when views clash, keep it cool; you don't have to agree with every opinion, just respect it and keep the cut moving.

Chapter Reflection Guide

4. Recall a moment you misread a client's slang, custom, or vibe. What did it teach you about tuning in to the community you serve?

____
____
____
____
____
____
____

5. Think back to a cut where you let the client do most of the talking. How did their body language or tone tell you they felt heard?

____
____
____
____
____
____
____

6. Remember a time a client's opinion clashed with yours. What helped you stay respectful, and how did that choice affect the relationship?

____
____
____
____
____
____
____

Setting Boundaries for After Hours

As a barber, maintaining control over your schedule is crucial for avoiding burnout and ensuring that your time is respected. Walk-in

clients who show up after hours can become a major inconvenience if you don't set clear boundaries from the start. While providing great service is important, so is making sure that your business runs on your terms.

Communicate your hours and fees clearly from the start. If you take a walk-in after closing, make sure they understand that this is not your normal schedule. Charge extra for after-hours cuts. Stand firm on your schedule. One of the most frustrating things is getting ready to leave, only to have a walk in show up and say, "Make me your last one." If you allow this, here's what will happen.

They assume you don't mind. They start bringing friends or kids with them after hours. They may tell others, leading to an increasing number of later night requests that you will eventually need to turn down.

You decrease your value as well if you don't charge extra for late services. You're working harder for the same pay, which lowers the value of your time.

You start feeling stressed and obligated instead of in control.

The earlier you establish boundaries, the easier it is to maintain them. If you allow after-hours walk-ins without rules, you'll struggle later when you try to enforce them. By doing this from the get-go, you can weed out the clients who don't respect your time while keeping the ones who truly value your service.

You are in control of your schedule; clients should not dictate it.

Your time outside the shop is just as important as your time in it. When you value your time, clients will too.

Setting after hours boundaries isn't just about protecting your schedule; it's about maintaining your mental and physical well-being.

Chapter Reflection Guide

1. When did you last stay late for a walk-in? Looking back, was the trade-off of time vs. pay worth it to you? Why or why not?

2. Write one clear, polite line you can use to explain after-hours fees or closing time the next time a client asks you to "squeeze them in."

3. Name one thing rest, family, hobby you'll protect by sticking to your set hours this month. How will you remind yourself why it matters?

Recreational Habits in the Barbershop

Some barbers have personal recreational habits, like smoking cannabis or drinking alcohol, but how you manage these habits in and around the shop can make or break your business.

In today's culture, smoking and drinking are common, but that doesn't mean everyone accepts them, especially in a professional setting like a barbershop.

Some clients won't say anything, but they will stop coming back.

Parents bringing their kids may not approve and won't return.

Your habits could affect the reputation of the shop, not just your chair.

Other barbers rely on the shop's image to make a living, and your actions could impact their business.

It's not about judgement; it's about being mindful that not everyone shares the same lifestyle. What you do in your personal time is your business, but

Once you step into the shop, your mindset should shift to being a professional.

Even if you step outside to smoke, be mindful of where and how you do it. Clients walking into a barbershop that smells like smoke may feel uncomfortable.

If your habits start causing issues with clients, you're not just affecting your own business; you're affecting the entire shop's success.

Not every barber or client shares the same habits. Keep your lifestyle separate from work and respect others' choices.

Your personal habits are just that personal. But when you're in the barbershop, it's not just about you; it's about the clients, the other barbers, and the business as whole.

Chapter Reflection Guide

1. Recall a moment you realized a personal habit (yours or another barber's) made a client uneasy. How did that experience reshape your understanding of professional boundaries?

   ____
   ____
   ____
   ____
   ____
   ____

2. Think of a time a single action smoke smell, open drink, off-color joke damaged, or could have damaged, the shop's image. What did that teach you about the impact of first impressions?

   ____
   ____
   ____
   ____
   ____
   ____
   ____

3. When you walk through the shop door, what thought or feeling lets you know it's "game time"? How can you strengthen that mental switch, so personal habits stay outside?

   ____
   ____
   ____
   ____
   ____
   ____
   ____

Why Undercutting Prices Hurts Your Career in the Long Run

Dropping your rates to pull in new heads feels smart at first, but it usually backfires. Cheap cuts fill the chairs, sure, yet those same clients bounce the second someone else undercuts you.

Meanwhile you're working harder for less cash, trimming corners on quality, and setting a price they'll expect forever. Hold your value better to charge what the work is worth and keep clients who respect the craft.

And not to mention the fact that doing this creates problems. Cheap clients are the hardest to do business with and the least loyal.

Bargain hunters also bring headaches. They're the toughest to please and their questions about why another barber costs more can stir up tension across the floor. If you're the only one charging less, the other barbers feel short-changed. Sooner or later, the owner will step in and either make you raise your prices or ask you to leave.

Many of these people are just looking for the cheapest option, not a long-term barber. If they see a lower price elsewhere, they'll leave just as

fast as they came. These aren't the type of clients you want to prioritize, nor as they the type of clients you want in your chair.

When they eventually see the real shop prices, they might feel overcharged or misled, leading to frustration and lost business.

A barbershop should have a consistent pricing structure that everyone respects, ensuring fairness.

Instead of competing with price, focus on skills, service, and professionalism.

Value your time. A strong barber focuses on quality over quantity, which leads to repeat business and higher-paying, loyal clients. Client's worth focusing on will recognize your value and pay your set price without bargaining.

Chapter Reflection Guide

1. Recall a time you lowered your price to win work. What did you learn about how others and you value your time and talent?

2. Picture two futures: one with fewer clients paying your full rate, and one with a steady flow of discounted clients. Which one would leave you feeling more energized and secure a year from now, and why?

3. If you commit to charging what your work is worth from today on, how could that choice shape your skills, finances, and reputation over the next two years?

Professionalism Over Everything

In this trade and in life, you'll hear a million different opinions some helpful, some just noise. Take them in with respect and consideration but always filter them through your own experience and instincts. Trusting your path and growth process. Significant improvement learning wisdom through the process from qualified experts and seasoned professionals and keeping company with people who push you forward. Seek out mentors and peers who are winning, both behind the chair and beyond it, and study the habits and discipline that set them apart. Advice is fine, but seeing those principles in action shows what really works. Build a circle that inspires and challenges you with real success. When you roll with folks who reach higher than average, their energy and understanding can lift your barbering and your life to the next level.

A strong barbershop culture rests on respect and professionalism. The shop is a place to do business, serve the community, and build genuine connections not to scout dates. When women come in whether they're clients booking their own cuts or moms bringing kids they deserve the same courtesy and focus as anyone else. Laughs and easy conversation are part of the vibe, but don't confuse friendly banter with romantic interest. Keep it professional, and you'll protect the welcoming atmosphere that keeps every client male or female coming back.

A major sign of maturity and professionalism as a barber is knowing how to separate business from personal interests. If a woman is a client of another barber, do not interfere with that relationship for personal gain. When a barber loses a client because another barber was pursuing them with no genuine intentions, it creates tension in the shop and disrupts business. No one wants to work alongside someone who is constantly jeopardizing their income for temporary pleasure.

This also applies to mothers who bring their children in for a haircut. A friendly smile or polite conversation does not automatically mean they are interested in you. Some barbers develop a reputation for being overly flirtatious, hitting on every female who walks in, or waiting outside the shop to make a move after their child's haircut. This behavior is unprofessional and makes the shop uncomfortable for both clients and fellow barbers.

If your name becomes associated with being "thirsty" for women in the shop, other barbers will stop trusting you around their female clients, and mothers will feel uncomfortable bringing their children in. This damages both your personal reputation and the shop's professional environment.

Remember, the barbershop is a place for business first. Your ability to control yourself, show respect, and maintain professionalism will determine how far you go in your career. Women appreciate barbers who treat them with respect rather than making them feel like a target. Keep your focus on providing great service and protecting the shop's reputation not your own personal desires.

Chapter Reflection Guide

1. Think of someone who inspires your growth. What's one move they make that you could apply in your own way this week?

2. Think of a time you mixed personal interest with work. How did it affect trust in the shop, and what boundary will you set from now on?

3. How will you show every client especially women and moms that your chair is a respectful, professional space?

Prioritizing the Client's Vision

One of the biggest lessons a barber must learn is that a great haircut doesn't mean a satisfied client. You can give a client a flawless fade, a clean lineup, and a smooth finish, but if it's not the haircut they envisioned, they won't be happy and that's what truly matters. In barbering, it's not about what you think looks best or what will get the most likes on social media; it's about delivering the haircut the paying client wants.

It's easy to take it personally when a client isn't completely satisfied, but this is part of the business. Instead of getting defensive, take a step back and listen. Did the client clearly explain what they wanted? Did you confirm before starting? Sometimes, miscommunication plays a role in the disconnect.

If the client is unhappy and you recognize that the misunderstanding was on your end, own it. In some cases, it might be worth refusing payment to maintain trust and show that you care about their satisfaction. Even if you disagree with their critique, keeping a professional attitude will go a long way. After all, they're the ones walking around with the haircut, so their opinion matters most.

Some ways to avoid these situations is to always start with a detailed consultation before picking up your clippers. Ask for specific's length, taper, fade, part, shape, and so on. Use reference photos to confirm their vision. Repeat what they said to ensure you're on the same page.

At the end of the day, barbering is a service industry. Your goal isn't just to give a great haircut; it's to give the client the haircut they want.

Chapter Reflection Guide

1. Ever had a client ask for something wild or unexpected?

2. Think back to a time when the cut didn't look like the picture the client showed you.

3. What simple step like showing a photo on your phone or repeating back what they asked for can you add to every consultation to make sure you and the client are on the same page?"

Building Trust & Integrity in the Barbershop

One quick way to ruin your reputation in the barbershop is to become the barber no one trusts the one who undercuts, schemes, and crosses boundaries by approaching another barber's clients instead of putting in the work to build clientele the right way. Every barber in the shop has put in time, effort, and consistency to earn their clients, and no one respects a barber who tries to shortcut the process at someone else's expense.

A common form of untrustworthy behavior is when a barber quietly markets their services to another barber's clients, passing out business cards, pitching additional services, or suggesting side deals while another barber is working hard to maintain their relationship with clients. For example, telling a client, "I do hair units with enhancements let me do your hair and your barber can just cut it" might seem like a business move, but it's disrespectful, unprofessional, and causes unnecessary tension in the shop. Clients should always have the freedom to choose their services, but when another barber is actively trying to redirect them for personal gain, it creates an environment of distrust and resentment.

When a barber builds a reputation for stealing clients, sidestepping professionalism, and taking advantage of the shop's traffic without contributing, it affects the entire shop dynamic. Other barbers won't respect or trust you; clients will pick up on the tension, and shop owners may start questioning your presence. While some shop owners may turn a blind eye just to ensure booth rent is paid, this kind of behavior can weaken the overall unity and integrity of the barbershop.

Instead of trying to munch off other barbers' clients, focus on building your own reputation through skill, professionalism, and trust. Attract clients the right way through quality cuts, exceptional service, and strong relationships.

Collaborate, don't compete unfairly. If you offer additional services, maintain a professional conversation and clear intentions. It's better to build ethical partnerships with barbers than to overstep by pursuing their clients. Respect every barber's effort. They've built their clientele through hard work, and they deserve the same respect you'd want for yourself.

Every barber in the barbershop deserves to work in an environment of mutual trust and respect. Build your clientele the right way, respect your peers, and establish a name that carries integrity not one that carries whispers of dishonesty.

Chapter Reflection Guide

1. Think of a time you considered approaching another barber's client, what's a smarter, more respectful move you could've made to grow your own clientele?

2. When a client sits in another barber's chair but chats with you, how do you keep the vibe friendly without overstepping?

3. What's one easy move like giving props on a clean cut or sending a client another barber's way that shows you're a team you're about growth, not ego?

Operating With an Ownership Mindset

We as barbers can make the mistake of putting all the responsibility on the shop owner and failing to recognize that success in this industry requires an ownership mindset, even when you don't own the shop. Whether you rent a booth or work on commission, you are still a business within a business. The way you handle your space, your clients, and your overall professionalism will determine how far you go in this field.

Don't wait for the owner to spell out every chore own it. Keep your station spotless and dialed in like your names on the lease; clients notice that pride and trust you more for it. Sweep the floor, empty the trash, restock the towels small moves that make the whole shop run smoother. And the job isn't just cutting hair: greet everyone who walks through the door, even if they never sit in your chair. Respect and initiative keep the place buzzing.

Market yourself as a business using social media, word of mouth, and promotions to attract clientele.

Keep your barber license current and invest in continuous education to stay updated with new techniques and industry trends.

While barbers are responsible for their individual success and maintaining a strong presence in the shop, the owner has their own set of responsibilities, like keeping the barbershop's business license up to date, ensuring utilities are paid, making sure everything functions properly, and creating an environment where every barber has an equal opportunity for growth. But just because the owner handles these aspects doesn't mean barbers should take the shop's upkeep for granted. It's a team effort.

Barbers who take responsibility for their space and their craft are the ones who see the most growth. When everyone in the shop operates with an ownership mentality, it creates a stronger, more successful business, be accountable, take pride in your work, and contribute to the shop's overall success.

Be the barber or shop owner who backs words with action. If something needs improving, step up instead of waiting for someone else to handle it. A solid shop runs on shared effort.

Trust runs the shop. Whether you're the first barber to unlock the door or the owner handling business, make sure the lights are on, key turns, barbershop license is current, and all bills are paid. No barber should show up one morning and discover the place is shutting down in a few weeks because someone let things slide.

Chapter Reflection Guide

1. What's one thing you can do at your station today to show clients this isn't just where you work it's your space, your brand?

____
____
____
____
____
____
____

2. What is one concrete step (social post, referral card,) you'll take this week to market yourself as a professional?

____
____
____
____
____
____
____

3. Think of something that would make the whole shop run smoother supplies, maintenance, morale. How will you take the lead on it instead of waiting for someone else?

____
____
____
____
____
____
____

Creating a Space

Writing this book forced me to make time where none existed. Shop days start early and end late, so I blocked out small pockets of time ten minutes before the first appointment, a quick moment after lunch, a half-hour before bed. While cutting I kept an earbud in one ear, listening to educational video. If a client drifted off, I opened the notes app and typed a few lines. At the gym, I logged ideas between sets, saving links to articles I planned to study later. Noise, exhaustion, and constant motion were obstacles, but carving out those pieces of time kept the pages moving forward.

The process reminded me how progress really happens in a barbershop. You master a clipper guard, then a taper, then a skin fades one focused session after another. Writing worked the same way: steady attention, no matter how small the window. There was never a perfect stretch of quiet or a fancy workspace waiting; there was just discipline, consistency, and a phone full of half-finished drafts slowly turning into chapters.

Clients, friends, and family saw that grind. They watched an idea turn into printed pages because I stayed on it every day. That outcome carries its own lesson: you don't need ideal conditions to change your life. You need a plan, the willingness to use every stray minute, and the patience to let small efforts pile up. When people you serve witness that kind of commitment whether it's perfecting their fade or finishing a book they start thinking bigger for themselves, too. And that's the impact you want to have long-term.

I intended for this book to guide you through the barbering journey, covering everything from building client relationships and maintaining professionalism. You've learned the importance of setting boundaries, adapting to different personalities, and staying mindful of your habits to create a successful and respected career. Whether it's accommodating elderly clients, walk-ins, or valuing your worth, each lesson is designed to help you navigate the industry with confidence.

Sections were created for you to have a space where you can write down your thoughts, perspectives, and experiences as you navigate the barber industry. As you grow, your mindset will evolve, and this will be a place to reflect on where you started, what you've learned, and where you're headed. One day, you'll look back at these pages and see your own growth, the lessons that shaped you, and the vision you're building for your future in barbering.

Final Thoughts

It all comes down to the vision of the barber. Whether your vision is big, moderate, or small, it's your idea your definition of success and what it looks like to you. At the end of the day, your greatness depends on you. It's about what you want to achieve and how you want to enjoy life with a peace of mind.

Maybe your goal is to be one of the best barbers in the industry, own the best shop in your city, or start a barber school. Maybe you see yourself as a social media educator, instructor, or running a podcast from the barbershop. You might want to own a mobile barber truck, a private suite, a loft, or cut hair from a high-rise balcony overlooking the city. Maybe your heart is in the community being that trusted barber in a small town, cutting hair outside in the park, by the beach, or in mountains for those scenic views. Some barbers link up with content creators in a creative house, building a barber channel together. Others create their own tools, products, carving out their own lane in the industry.

Full-time or part-time, whatever you choose, own it. Give it your all and go for it. Just imagine holding your clippers and realizing that everything you've ever dreamed of every goal you've set is being achieved as you hold a clipper in the palm of your hand and turn on the power. Your barbering journey is yours to create.

www.ingramcontent.com/pod-product-compliance
Lightning Source LLC
LaVergne TN
LVHW061224100826
845148LV00004B/858

* 9 7 9 8 2 1 8 5 8 9 3 3 2 *